Ginkgo Gold

HAIKU
SOCIETY OF
AMERICA

Ginkgo Gold

HSA Members' Anthology
2025

Edited by Nicky Gutierrez

Title: Ginkgo Gold

Editor: Guiterrez, Nicky

ISBN: 978-1-930172-27-2 (paperback)

Published in the United States of America.

Design Layout: Nicky Guiterrez

Cover Design: Crystal Simone Smith

Introduction

Dear haiku friends,

In your hands is the HSA Member's Anthology 2025!

Thank you all for sending in your work! It has been a joy seeing how wonderful and talented our members are and how haiku has grown in the last few years. Without your submissions and dedication to the art of haiku and HSA, this anthology would not exist.

I thank our president, Crystal Simone Smith, and the HSA executive committee for entrusting me with this task. I am grateful to give back to the community that has given so much to me in my haiku journey.

It was an honor, privilege, and blessing to work on the anthology. This project has also been a joy and learning experience. So much kindness and charity have been given to me through this process, and I thank everyone for bearing with me during this time.

The anthology title comes from Dian Duchin Reed's poem "ginkgo gold." There is something magical about when the ginkgo leaves turn gold. To me, the ginkgo leaf is one of the quintessential symbols of haiku.

There are so many amazing haiku in this anthology that I know you will enjoy reading. By God's grace this anthology is finished, and I pray that it will be a blessing to you. Thank you!

In haiku,

Nicky Gutierrez

corn country
trucks idle below
rest stop stars[1]

Curtis Alan

telegram
his grandmere's
drowned spectacles[2]

Melanie Alberts

who says the world is fleeting   river rock[3]

Rupa Anand

[1] *The Heron's Nest* Volume XXVII, Number 1
[2] *Failed Haiku* Vol. 9, Issue 100
[3] *FemkuMag*, Issue 38

summer morning
grinding the coffee beans
for a fresh cup

Barbara Mosbacher Anderson

stargazer lilies
the heady scent
of second chances[4]

Cynthia Anderson

cloud cover
the sun rises
without her

Christine Aquilino

---

[4] *tsuri-dōrō #22*

summer's end
the sound of a cricket
in the kitchen[5]

Eric Arthen

out of the blue —
breathtaking clouds
of blackthorn blossom[6]

Vicky Arthurs

first day of summer
mosquito finds a hole
in my window screen

Kathi Ashmore

---

[5] *New England Letters*, 132
[6] *Blithe Spirit* 35.2

peppering the sky
with their departure
swallow wings[7]

Joanna Ashwell

steamy night
of wild dancing—
fireflies[8]

Evelyn Atreya

shift of shade
under a yucca
el norte

Steve Bahr

---

[7] *The Solitary Daisy*, Issue 37
[8] *Modern Haiku* 55.3

peach blossoms
at Shiloh, bright pink
the men who died there[9]

Jo Balistreri

empty nest
the porch light
stays on[10]

Michelle Ballou

DEI
Latin lesson
noted[11]

Caroline Giles Banks

[9] *Modern Haiku* 55.3
[10] *Kingfisher*, Issue 10
[11] *bottle rockets* #50

giving itself
to the greater go(o)d
raindrop[12]

Francine Banwarth

in the hollows
of a popped flyaway
spent-petalled rain

John Barlow

rippling wind a fox runs the ridge[13]

Dyanna Basist

---

[12] *Modern Haiku* 55.1
[13] *Wales Haiku Journal Winter* 2023-2024

ending my day on a high note red-winged blackbird[14]

Sam Bateman

sunflower face shines
passion blooms in my garden
simply there joy is

Susan K Beard

the shift to passive voice planet earth[15]

Roberta Beary

[14] *tinywords*, Issue 24.2
[15] *The Heron's Nest* Volume XXVI, Number 4

southward bound
the rising sweetness
of drying tobacco[16]

Lori Becherer

falling seed husks
one more cardinal
before dusk[17]

Brad Bennett

spring rain
overhead
a rug is beaten

Jerome Berglund

---

[16] *The Heron's Nest* Volume XXVI, Number 4
[17] *Plums's 2025 Haiku Competition, first place*

ribbons of rubber on the road leaving town[18]

Sally Biggar

sea spray
two buckets
of rose hips[19]

Shawn Blair

a circle of stones
most wildflowers
kept in

Randy Brooks

[18] *The Heron's Nest,* Volume XXVI, Number 1
[19] *Upstate Dim Sum* 2024/I

drive slowly
no need to hurry--
yellow forsythia

Daniel W. Brown

first day of spring
   rain braided
         with snow

Roberta Brown

airport layover
no flights to
an ascetic future[20]

Kevin Browne

---

[20] *Five Fleas*, March 17, 2025

morning fog
the suggestion
of trees[21]

Chris Bruner

still mountain pond
the only sound
snow

Robert Bruntil

end of journey
flecks of alfalfa
on an erratic rock

John Budan

---

[21] *The Heron's Nest*, Volume XXVII, Number 1

elusive word
a summer cloud forms
then evaporates

Alanna C. Burke

hunger moon
an unmarked scenic overlook[22]

Eric Burke

the piano she played still the lilacs[23]

Marylyn Burridge

---

[22] *Modern Haiku* 54.3
[23] *Modern Haiku* 55.3

city night--
white moths tango
over the trash[24]

Sondra J. Byrnes

autumn rain
journaling
my gray clouds[25]

Claire Vogel Camargo

temple bell . . .
the single stroke
of an enso[26]

Theresa A. Cancro

---

[24] *Creatrix* (#69)
[25] *Akitsu Quarterly* Fall/Winter 2024
[26] *The Bamboo Hut*, February 2024

morning moon
a dragonfly follows
my gaze

Matthew Caretti

outside my window
the tree extends
its branch[27]

Patricia Carragon

the red veins
of an okra blossom
autumn equinox

Anna Cates

---

[27] *Wales Haiku Journal*, Autumn 2024

hometown
the lingering tang
of candied ginger[28]

Antoinette Cheung

back to nature
bison burgers
on the gas grill[29]

Thomas Chockley

forest bathing—
after the robin's song
clap of thunder

Margaret Chula

[28] *First Frost* 8
[29] Modern Haiku 51.1

under umbrella
waiting
rain drumming

John Paul Ciarrocchi

the ongoing foot
of the slug—leaves me
with glistening thoughts[30]

Rick Clark

blood moon
from midnight photo shoot
my bone white fingers

Marcyn Del Clements

---

[30] Mukai Farm Haiku Contest, third place

the ones left behind river stones[31]

Glenn G. Coats

seek or seek not still
nothing remains hidden long
upon shallow shore

Lee Cobert

where I return
his ashes to the stars
phosphorescent sea[32]

Wendy Cobourne

---

[31] *Frogpond* 48:1
[32] *Presence Haiku Journal* no. 81

crystal perfection
flows under a jaundice sky,
whispers of Monday breeze

Carlos Colon-Ortiz

day after Easter
silence of the church
just a priest and his broom[33]

Howard Colyer

diving for paua
deeper and deeper
the sound of blue[34]

Sue Courtney

---

[33] Blithe Spirit 34.2
[34] *A Sensory Journey: Haiku Down Under Anthology 2024*

my old street
memories cast shadows
I cannot touch[35]

Dina E. Cox

battery low
switching to
real life[36]

Tim Cremin

one year sober
a dozen roses
in a wine bottle[37]

Alvin B. Cruz

[35] *Porch to Porch A Maritime Haiku Anthology 2024*
[36] *Acorn* no. 54: Spring 2025
[37] *Cold Moon Journal*, Jan. 2, 2025

in season watermelon emojis[38]

Daniel Shank Cruz

pear trees
winter snowflakes
fluctuate

Patricia Cruzan

a snowball
in my cupped hands
winter moon[39]

Maya Daneva

---

[38] *Acorn* no. 52: Spring 2024
[39] *Blithe Spirit* 34.1

revelation
the day the sun became
a star[40]

Pat Davis

dog days
an invitation to join
the neighborhood watch[41]

Cherie Hunter Day

reverse side
of a woollen cardigan
her mom all her life[42]

Bipasha Majumder De

[40] *Akitsu Quarterly* Fall/Winter 2024
[41] *First Frost* 9
[42] *Wales Haiku Journal*, Winter 2023-2024

just off my bow
two dolphins sail over
a plagiarized moon

Jim DeLong

                                blue skies
the shadow of a raptor
        on ice[43]

Melissa Dennison

street-fighting . . .
face to face
the crows bicker[44]

Charlotte Digregorio

[43] *Blue: A Humana Obscura Anthology*
[44] *The Haiku Foundation Volunteers Anthology 2024*

neither coming nor going winter fly[45]

Karen DiNobile

neighbors frolic
uninvited in our pool
feathers left behind

Mimi Dollinger

winter sun —
a crabapple disappears
peck by peck[46]

Janice Doppler

---

[45] *Modern Haiku* 55.1
[46] *The Cicada's Cry*, Winter 2024

parking lot lights shine
a painting on the asphalt
as the sunlight fades

Simon Dorfman

airport parting
her wave
follows me[47]

Hans C. Dringenberg

a flock of juncos
could be mistaken for stones
on a withered field

Stuart Dumais

---

[47] *NO TWO alike: Haiku Canada Members' Anthology 2024*

elysium…
in your seasoned palm
a robin pecking seed[48]

for poet Michael Longley

Tim Dwyer

warbler high in tree
drunk
on its own plum song

Flora Inez Eberhart

fleeting sunshine —
with one stroke of the pen
I disappear with you

Robert Epstein

---

[48] *Blithe Spirit* 35.1

here – alone
the shape of your absence
fills me[49]

Robert Erlandson

old wooden stump
my grandson trades
one lap for another[50]

Julie Ann Espinoza

what I just can't grasp stinging nettle

Eavonka Ettinger

---

[49] *DailyHaiga,* May 27, 2020
[50] *Modern Haiku* 56.1

this year
the mesquite tree blooms
dragonflies[51]

Jackson Ercil Evans

grebes mating
the song and dance
we make of it[52]

Keith Evetts

committee meeting
the art of
chewing water[53]

Mike Fainzilber

---

[51] *Frogpond* 48.2
[52] *Modern Haiku* 55:3
[53] *tsuri-dōrō* #27

history lesson
ancient olive trees
still ripe with fruit

Elizabeth Fanto

clinging to erect sea cucumber
octopus leers and scans coral
for more drifting salad

Frances Farrell

the bending
of a rainbow …
spring wildflowers[54]

Barbara Feehrer

---

[54] *Modern Haiku* 55.3

migrating geese
my father loses
his words

Nancy Fernandez

longleaf pine
reading the fascicle
"being-time" a tenth time[55]

Thomas Festa

night train
in his pocket
she tucks a love note

Joan C. Fingon

---

[55] *Modern Haiku* 55.3

while
you were gone
wasp nest[56]

Denise Fontaine-Pincince

Summer afternoon
  a Bach flute sonata
    cools the air[57]

Sylvia Forges-Ryan

a patch of violets—
beyond its margin
more violets

Mark Forrester

---

[56] *2024 Hexapod Haiku Challenge, honorable mention*
[57] *Chrysanthemum* Issue 32

zen painting class
the freedom of not being
very good[58]

Robert Forsythe

morning sun
the snow melt
between pine shadows

Jay Friedenberg

over the beach
clouds cover constellations
starfish

Cynthia Gallaher

---

[58] *Something Left: Towpath Anthology, 2025*

slow pulse
of engine idle—we learn
how we must wait[59]

Dianne Garcia

this time
i want to believe him
winter aconites[60]

Susan Godwin

Japanese kites
admiring their reflections
in the koi pond[61]

Captain Billy Sayles / Oliver Gold

---

[59] *Glimmering Hour: Northwest 35th Anniversary Anthology*
[60] *2025 Wisconsin Poet's Calendar*
[61] *Drawing and Haiku The Art of Zen Maintenance*

even the sheep
I am counting
are falling asleep

Connie Goodman-Milone

the graveyard
so many dead
stars in the sky[62]

LeRoy Gorman

small fingers
scolded to *andante*
blossoms in the window[63]

Adam Graham

---

[62] *cattails*, April 2023
[63] *Kingfisher*, Issue 11

the hunter's moon
and my breath
on the windshield[64]

Sari Grandstaff

a friend request
from a dead relative
flickering street light[65]

John S Green

washing its hands
in the garden koi pond—
the old raccoon[66]

Steven H. Greene

---

[64] *The Mainichi Daily Haiku* in English Jan. 8, 2025
[65] *Failed Haiku*, Vol. 9, issue 97
[66] New Jersey Botanical Garden, April 2025

snow falling on pines
the breath before
he says my name[67]

Margie Gustafson

last prayer
the dirt
between my toes[68]

Nicky Gutierrez

each year the same
each year different
magnolias in bloom[69]

Johnnie Johnson Hafernik

---

[67] *Leaf* Issue Six March 2025
[68] *Kingfisher*, Issue 10
[69] *Modern Haiku* 55:2

sunlight
where it never was before
downed sycamore

Maureen Lanagan

antique water can
morning reminder
of daytime chores

Tonya Hall

still life
covering my drawing
with layers

Joy Hallinan

Now narrowing path
navigates a gnarly root.
Nimbly melting snow.

Dana Hallman

whale fall
my ocean's quiet
deaths[70]

Jennifer Hambrick

whispering lake winds wash over paw prints through dunes the clink of a chain

Catharine Summerfield Hāna

---

[70] *Heliosparrow Haiku Frontier Awards 2024, Heliosparrow Poetry Journal, first place*

iridescence of a whelk shell exposed

Jon Hare

for just a moment
the universe
in a sunflower[71]

Charles Harmon

reincarnation
cherries budding over
headstones[72]

Lev Hart

---

[71] *Akitsu Quarterly* Spring/Summer 2024
[72] *Sakura Haiku Challenge*, Consulate General of Japan in Toronto, May 2024

the ones who sit
the ones who stand…
Veteran's Day[73]

Michele L. Harvey

spring afternoon
at his gravesite
she reads to him

Patricia Harvey

family photo
my mom
still smiling[74]

Quamrul Hassan

---

[73] *Modern Haiku* 55:2
[74] *Modern Haiku* 56:2

banished to my room
I discover
poetry[75]

Shasta Hatter

lighting a lantern
on a wheeled stand —
Ramadan dusk

Akihiko Hayashi

glissando
warm wind
across mussel shells[76]

Kathryn P. Haydon

---

[75] *Failed Haiku*, Vol. 9, Issue 102
[76] *Wales Haiku Journal*, Summer 2024

burnt olive grove
the cry
of hungry winds[77]

Betsy Hearne

before and after
cherry blossoms
the soft forgetting[78]

Karin Hedetniemi

river's bend
two moons
settling in[79]

Deborah Burke Henderson

[77] *Modern Haiku* 55:3
[78] Best of British Columbia, *2024 Haiku Invitational*, Vancouver Cherry Blossom Festival
[79] *Chrysanthemum* Issue 32

bayou night
part of the galaxy
the gator's eyes[80]

Frank Higgins

winter sunset
she trades her rack
of scrabble tiles

Merle D. Hinchee

pulling a cold one
from the spring house
red salamander[81]

Jeff Hoagland

---

[80] *The Heron's Nest* Volume XXVII, Number 1
[81] *tsuri-dōrō* #21

measuring
the length of another day
green inchworm

Ruth Holzer

glow of my watch dial
this would have been
his birthday[82]

Frank Hooven

gentle rain
in young grass an old sheepskin
cuddles its bones[83]

Christine Horner

---

[82] *Modern Haiku* 55:2
[83] *GEPPO* L:1 Feb. 2025

cumuli tumbling
above strollers in a park
the blackbirds of Amsterdam

Marshall Hryciuk

crumbling church
wisteria takes
the pulpit[84]

Edward Cody Huddleston

no matter
how many magpies
still a blank page[85]

Lee Hudspeth

---

[84] *Illinois State Poetry Society's Modern Haiku Awards*, 2024,
1st Prize
[85] *Kingfisher*, Issue 10

a frosty night
in sunny California
shattered illusions

Gil Jackofsky

yellow boots
and streetlights
stay on all day

Rick Jackofsky

morning sun
crane unfolds itself
origami

Roberta Beach Jacobson

relocation
of a flower pot
roly-polies unroll[86]

Sharon Rhutasel Jones

brother's silver flute
shapes the wind
mixed yard birds gather

Stephen R. Jones

crying child...
the wet nurse offers
the other breast[87]

Hans Jongman

---

[86] *Modern Haiku* 56:1
[87] *Congeries – Poems by Hans Jongman*

clear water
a school of fish
hiding, unhiding

Deborah Karl-Brandt

Saydnaya's monasteries
to the abandoned prison yard
dandelion fluff descends

Bassem AL Kassem

frost
overnight
a key change[88]

David J. Kelly

---

[88] *Acorn* no. 52: Spring 2024

pebbled path
dusk
still bathed in sunlight

Jill Kessler

no one died today
funeral directors stand
watching passing cars[89]

Howard Lee Kilby

homecoming:
everywhere the orange flutterings
of butterflies newly born

Aijung Kim

---

[89] *Modern Haiku*, Spring 1995

an agitating wind
   red samara has joined me
      on the bench

Jodi King

autumn breeze
each leaf with its own
flight path

Ravi Kiran

thousands of people
left behind
in his library[90]

Michael Kitchen

---

[90] *failed haiku*, Vol. 6, Issue 67

old growth
a forest within
city limits[91]

Deb Koen

I don't want to let go
the last leaf
to fall[92]

Yvette Nicole Kolodji

Georgia O'K
plays the Blues
on Canvas

Edward Kosiewicz

[91] *The Heron's Nest*, Volume XXVI, Issue 1
[92] *Akitsu-Quarterly* Fall/Winter, 2024

star paths
tracing the lines
on Grandma's quilt[93]

Kimberly Kuchar

last thing touched
before she left
shriveled flowers

Michael Lamb

in drizzle greyness
the red spot
of a hairy woodpecker[94]

Jill Lange

---

[93] Presence *Haiku Journal* no. 78
[94] *cattails*, October 2024

what my neighbors
want me to know
little free library[95]

Jim Laurila

moving day
i wrap my dishes
in news of war[96]

Sarah Lawhorne

page turner
the breeze
gets ahead of me[97]

Suzanne Leaf-Brock

---

[95] *Modern Haiku* 56:1
[96] *Failed Haiku*, Vol. 10, Issue 106
[97] *Chrysanthemum* Issue 33

gorging on blackberries
a flock of waxwings
spiral out of control

Michael Henry Lee

thunder claps echo
rain drops collect on asphalt
hydroplane action

Venessa Y. Lee-Estevez

growing old
together
the cat and I

Brenda Lempp

boatyard storage
the shrink-wrapped ghosts
of winter[98]

Barrie Levine

the cadence of fairy tales thistle dusk[99]

Kathryn Liebowitz

wrensong —
wood frog embryos
wriggle in their eggs[100]

Kristen Lindquist

---

[98] *Haiku in Action*, January 2024
[99] *The Heron's Nest* Volume XXVII, Number 1
[100] *The Heron's Nest* Volume XXVI, Number 3

slanted moonlight
on a half-collapsed school wall
chalk poppies bloom[101]

Chen-ou Liu

October dawn
on the garden dahlia
a honeybee face up[102]

Cyndi Llyod

neighbor's yard
three brown butterflies
braid the air[103]

Amy Losak

---

[101] *NeverEnding Story*, August 3, 2024
[102] *Frogpond* 47:3
[103] *Wing Strokes Haiku*

the whole of history
in an appendix
autumn wind[104]

Patricia J. Machmiller

corn tassels
rustle in the wind
Mum's taffeta dress[105]

Lillian Nakamura Maguire

unfamiliar birdsong—
when I whistle it
the cat sits up[106]

C. R. Manley

---

[104] *The Heron's Nest* Volume XXVI, Number 1
[105] *Haiku Canada Review*, Oct. 2023, Vol. 17 #2
[106] *Glimmering Hour: Haiku Northwest 35th Anniversary Anthology*

getting nosy the neighbor's lilacs[107]

Matthew Markworth

finally
not checking my phone
summer stars[108]

Jeannie Martin

high school again
another lesson
on mood rings[109]

Richard L. Matta

---

[107] *The Heron's Nest* Volume XXVI, Number 3
[108] *Frogpond* 47.2
[109] *bottle rockets* #52

last days of winter
a refreshed earth awakens
with beginner's eyes

Kathleen McAllen

daydreaming words in the creek's babble[110]

Mary McCormack

snowfall
throughout the night
Marley's chains[111]

Joe McKeon

---

[110] *Trying on the Night Sky*
[111] *Katonah Poetry Series*, 1st place

dusty access road
zinnia & fish guts
rise to the sunshine

Forest Meadow

the night leaving
all the dreams
inside my eyes[112]

Rita R. Melissano

collecting sea glass . . .
I carry home
the deepest blue[113]

MJ Mello

[112] *Heliosparrow Poetry Journal*, August 31, 2024
[113] *folk ku journal* issue 4

treehouse
the one password
I remember[114]

Sarah E. Metzler

hell-flower
the ghost of you
still in my hollow[115]

Rowan Beckett Minor

thinking out loud
a spider hangs
from the ceiling lamp

Mike Montreuil

---

[114] *The Heron's Nest* Volume XXVI, Number 3
[115] *tsuri-dōrō* #21

wet road home
toward the rainbow
radio Gospel[116]

Lenard D. Moore

shipyard cranes
loom over mountains
the stories we tell[117]

Ross Moore

oh mosquitoes. . .
so much depends
on the old pond[118]

Wilda Morris

---

[116] *The Heron's Nest,* Volume XXVI, Number 2
[117] *NOON: journal of the short poem,* issue 26
[118] *Trash Panda,* vol. 5

re-phrasing
the question
fiddlehead ferns[119]

Laurie D. Morrissey

thoughts shrouded in mist,
absently her fingers
stroke the cat[120]

Sherri J. Moye-Dombrosky

azure sky
the scent of pine resin
along the trail[121]

Leanne Mumford

---

[119] *The Heron's Nest* Volume XXVI Number 3
[120] *Haiku in Action*, March 2, 2025
[121] *Seashores* 12

a moment with leaves
not yet yellow
frogs sleep in the mud

Debra Murphy

bright sunlight peeking
onto frigid white blanket
three coats of fur lay

Linda Nash

after a spring storm
alders tumbling into
a familiar path

Beth Nauman-Montana

my dad -
out standing in his field
one last time[122]

Melissa Leaf Nelson

moonlit cloud...
the test results
can wait

Stephanie Newbern

plated flower
feasting
hummingbird[123]

Suzanne Niedzielska

---

[122] *Mayfly* Issue 76
[123] *Nor'easter* May 2025

trendy at last
my eco-friendly
dandelion lawn[124]

Catherine Anne Nowaski

how many steps
walked today
evensong[125]

William O'Sullivan

porch light on
for my lost daughter
only moths come[126]

Mary Oishi

---

[124] *Modern Haiku* 56.1
[125] *Presence Haiku Journal* no. 79
[126] *Cholla Needles* 97

early Sunday
silence and sun
gardens grow[127]

Ellen Grace Olinger

in nana's yard
catching fireflies
with his brother

Robert Oliveira

driving rain —
snug under a lone pine
the scent of sheep[128]

Ben Oliver

---

[127] *Journal Notes Blog* 2025
[128] *Under the basho* (3/31/25)

water's edge
a sun-baked footprint
harbors a feather[129]

Debbie Olson

soft notes unfurling fiddleheads[130]

Nancy Orr

enough
to water the wildflowers
first rains[131]

Renée Owen

---

[129] *Frogpond* 47.2
[130] *Modern Haiku* 55:3
[131] *Modern Haiku* 55.2

city dawn
high-rise windows
heave the sun[132]

Roland Packer

church bells
the bucket's
first berries[133]

John Pappas

monastery fountain
I can't remember
what I wished for[134]

Sarah Paris

---

[132] *Presence Haiku Journal* no. 81
[133] *The Heron's Nest* Volume XXVI, Number 2
[134] *Hedgerow* #146

paper making the poetics of wasps[135]

Marianne Paul

ocean sounds
of a Houston freeway
morning zazen[136]

James A. Paulson

umbrella banyan
outspread now these sunny days--
will drape my ashes[137]

James Penha

[135] *Whiptail: journal of the single line poem*, Issue 9
[136] *the smell of leaves*: buddha baby press
[137] *Asahi Haikuist Network*, January 3, 2025

the bounce of hailstones--
jumping bean memories
pop up

Ann M. Penton

a thousand leaves
with the wind
tango

Andrew Pineo

falling leaves
the gentle pulse
of the oxygen tank[138]

Marilyn Powell

---

[138] *Frogpond* 47:3

blossom arch
the flutter of waxwings
dusty with pollen[139]

Vanessa Proctor

mountains cradle
a sea of daffodils
nature's halo

Kathryn Pumphrey

September gold finch
what marigolds remain

Dianne Puterbaugh

---

[139] *Presence Haiku Journal* no. 81

twilight breeze the swish of a black horse's tail

Katherine Raine

a day's work
in her apron pocket
scraps of jotted poems[140]

Holli Rainwater

ginkgo gold
spent in one night
autumn wind[141]

Dian Duchin Reed

---

[140] *Wales Haiku Journal,* Autumn 2024
[141] *The Heron's Nest* Volume XXVII, Number 1

spring stream
she lifts the saree
just enough[142]

Meera Rehm

middle age
not enough wind
for the kite[143]

Dave Reynolds

robin's eggshell picking up the sky[144]

Susanna Rich

[142] *Acorn* Issue #50
[143] *Presence Haiku Journal* no. 81
[144] *The Heron's Nest* Volume XXVI, Number 3

autumn wildflowers
their last act
of seed making

Bryan Rickert

at-home hospice
each day
the house shrinks[145]

Edward J. Rielly

a few red leaves
on the crepe myrtle
his torn kite[146]

Barbara Robinette

---

[145] *First Frost #9*
[146] *Ouachita Life*, Honorable Mention, December 2022

mayflies . . .
casting a line the length
of my lunch hour[147]

Chad Lee Robinson

the widow's mailbox
suddenly full
of bluebirds[148]

Daniel Robinson

soothing my late night neurons pemberley[149]

Michele Root-Bernstein

---

[147] *The Heron's Nest*, Volume XXVI, Number 2
[148] *Modern Haiku* 55.3
[149] *Frogpond* 47:2

Year of the Snake
I shed
my shame

Ce Rosenow

first cup of coffee
a daylily opens
just a crack[150]

Nicholas H. Rossler

sunbathing
a laughing gull
splats on my back

Raymond C. Roy

---

[150] *The Heron's Nest* Volume XXVII, Number 1

chrysanthemums
their shadows a little longer
a little sooner[151]

Suraja Menon Roychowdhury

a sudden stillness
among the birds
hawk shadow

Maggie Roycraft

silence
I'm drifting away . . .
a paper boat

Lidia Rozmus

---

[151] *haikuKATHA* (36), 2024

wisps of fog adrift on the river two mergansers[152]

Janet Ruth

still awake
ruminating
two owls weigh in

Ellen Ryan

ritual
running the burnt match
under water[153]

Tom Sacramona

---

[152] *Cold Moon Journal* 4/10/25
[153] *Akitsu Quarterly* Spring/Summer 2025

tangled ivy . . .
the hidden faces
of a sequoia[154]

Jacob D. Salzer

crunch time
I ditch a date
with my deadline[155]

Bona 'M. Santos

deep drought
a dab of perfume
on the rainmaker's wrist[156]

Kelly Sargent

[154] *Presence Haiku Journal* no. 81
[155] *Poetry Pea Podcast* 8/2024
[156] *Frogpond* 47:3

spring freeze
his passwords stuck
in the cloud

Cam Sato

small town signs
snow fills the crevices
of kanji[157]

Agnes Eva Savich

dry January
shots of whipped cream
straight from the can[158]

Michelle Schaefer

---

[157] *Seashores* 14
[158] *Prune Juice* Issue #46

collection basket
the price
of forgiveness[159]

Bonnie J Scherer

wild iris
the years before we knew her
as grandma[160]

Rich Schilling

diary
yesterday's entry
today's aha

Karen E. Schlumpp

---

[159] *Akitsu Quarterly* Spring/Summer 2025
[160] *The Heron's Nest* Volume XXVI, Number 1

milkweed moon
my chrysalis
splits[161]

Ann K. Schwader

Sabbath breeze…
the apple tree puts a little more
in the offering[162]

Dan Schwerin

Pentecost red
the azalea speaking
fluent finch[163]

Julie Schwerin

---

[161] *Modern Haiku* 55.3
[162] *Wales Haiku Journal* Summer, 2024
[163] *Modern Haiku* 56.1

first light
the farmer finishing
a rain-washed pear

Paula Sears

color of the sun
pressed into earth,
a maple leaf[164]

Katrina Serwe

anthropocene—
the call of whales
silenced[165]

Elizabeth Shack

[164] *Cold Moon Journal*, November 18, 2024
[165] *The Haiku Foundation's Haiku Dialogue*, 4/30/25

abandoned farm …
in the empty pasture
milkweeds

George Skane

stretch marks
I touch up
an old canvas

Crystal Simone Smith

hottest day
sea otters play
in kelp forest shade

Lyle Smith

lightning strike
scorched surge protector
did its duty

Michael K. Smith

my heart flutters the swallowtail's torn wings[166]

Matt Snyder

raven atop
the towering snag --
a winter's tale[167]

Sheila Sondik

---

[166] *Akitsu Quarterly,* Spring/Summer 2025
[167] *tinywords* Issue 24/1

playing
the blues—
wolf pack

Lisa Sparaco

fallen leaves
on my porch
a thousand haiku

Evan Spivack

public park
shopping cart lady
collecting good mornings[168]

Sandra St-Laurent

---

[168] *Morioka 3rd Haiku Contest*, Japan 2021, Honorable
Mention,

sea dunes
my father's hands
writing this

Joshua St. Claire

grand piano . . .
her aging hands
playing their song

Stephenie Story

making rent—
in the corner web
another fly[169]

Dylan Stover

---

[169] *Failed Haiku*, Issue 99

refugee train
small hands starfished
against the glass[170]

Debbie Strange

nursing home –
walker next to the bed
has cobwebs on it

Lee Strong, OFS

party in full swing—
silent in one corner,
an upright piano

Dean Summers

---

[170] Triveni Haiku Awards, 1st Place, 2024

the last summer
on analog time
hickory slingshot

Eric Sundquist

colorless palette
with its wings soaring
above this campus

Ryoko M. Suzuki

coldest night
cat belly
warming mine[171]

Carol Tagstrom

---

[171] *bottle rockets* #51,

children's footprints
around a puddle
spawning frogs[172]

Rick Tarquinio

skimming stones...
trying to recall
his holding hand[173]

Herb Tate

walking home
after a night of partying
the hoot owl still hooting[174]

Margaret Tau

---

[172] *cattails*, April 2024
[173] *Modern Haiku* 55.1
[174] *Frogpond* 47:2

reaching
for the sky
star jasmine[175]

Leon Tefft

rough around the edges morning moon[176]

Angela Terry

daybreak
the rustle of bats roosting
in a shagbark hickory[177]

Jennifer Thiermann

---

[175] *tsuri-doro* #23
[176] *tsuri-doro* #25
[177] *Mariposa* 51 Autumn/Winter 2024

summer visit
peeling the lichen off
my father's name

Ken Thompson

alone in field
turkey fans tail feathers
no mate in sight

T. A. Thorfinnson

igneous rock—
sunset falls
with the plunging water[178]

Richard Tice

---

[178] *cattails*, October 2024

first light -
this time my scan says
the thinkable[179]

Xenia Tran

scar tissue . . .
the cherry tree blossoms
outside her window

Kevin Valentine

after the storm
moon and
white roses

beverly verner

[179] *Autumn Moon Haiku Journal* 7:2, Spring/Summer 2024

automatic doors
    the toddler
        tests the magic[180]

Diane Wallihan

old team photo ...
once again
the last one chosen

Lew Watts

filtered sun
a dragonfly explores
an open page of Issa[181]

Joseph P. Wechselberger

---

[180] *Kingfisher*, Issue 9
[181] *Leaf*, Issue 5

end of winter season ---
kids splashing
in the old village fountain

Adèle Weers

sun's reflection
a perfect disk
on the slow stream

Mary Weidensaul

spring cleaning—
a little sand
escapes from the conch

Michael Dylan Welch

grief journal
she edits
the punctuation[182]

Christine Wenk-Harrison

despite the wind
a squirrel goes
out on a limb

Caroline Wermuth

long drive
a check engine light
shines in the dark

Allyson Whipple

---

[182] *Prune Juice*, Issue # 44

blue skies, light dapples
through green buds - dead leaves
glowing, ground awakening

Robin White

as if snow
on mountains weren't enough--
cant of light[183]

Scott Wiggerman

above the pond
and in the pond
one firefly[184]

Kayla Wildman

---

[183] *Akitsu Quarterly,* Spring/Summer 2024
[184] *Haiku in Action*, December 13, 2024

her delight in
finding losing
finding a frog[185]

Tony Williams

cicada hatching in our own time[186]

Valorie Broadhurst

helium balloon
tied around a toddler's wrist
momentarily[187]

Alison Woolpert

[185] *Blithe Spirit,* 34.3
[186] *password,* issue 2:1
[187] *Geppo,* Feb. '25

last day of school
the slow hush
of closing books

Nitu Yumnam

fallen flower
in rain
— picked

Dhru

the vesak moon
playing hide and seek…
with festive lanterns!

JoyPoet

wildfire smoke
at midday
one street light turns on[188]

kjmunro

shadows
of a chainmail fence
mark off the sidewalk

Nemuko

---

[188] *Mayfly* 76, Winter 2024